LEARNING GERMAN FOR SCHOOL STUDENTS

DR DHEERAJ MEHROTRA

Contents

Preface   *v*

1. The German Alphabet   1

2. Numbers And Counting   11

3. Common Phrases In German   23

4. Asking For Directions   38

5. At A Restaurant   47

6. 100 Most Common Vocabulary   64

7. 100 Commonly Used Sentences   79

Books By The Same Author   95

Preface

German is one of Europe's most widely spoken languages, and mastering it can benefit academic, professional, and personal growth. This book provides a step-by-step approach to learning German, starting with fundamental vocabulary and gradually progressing to essential grammar, sentence structures, and everyday conversations. The lessons are carefully designed to be student-friendly, making learning both effective and enjoyable.

This book includes Basic greetings and introductions to help you start conversations confidently—common phrases for daily life, travel, and school interactions. Essential grammar rules are explained in a simple and comprehensible manner. Engaging exercises and practice activities to reinforce learning. Cultural insights to help students appreciate the German-speaking world. We aim to make learning German accessible and enjoyable for school students.

By the end of this book, learners will have developed a strong foundation in the language, allowing them to communicate effectively in various situations. We encourage students to practice regularly, immerse themselves in German culture, and, most importantly, enjoy the process of learning. With dedication and enthusiasm, mastering German will become a rewarding experience.

Happy learning!

Author

ONE
THE GERMAN ALPHABET

The German Alphabet

The German alphabet is a fascinating aspect of the German language. It consists of 26 letters, similar to the English alphabet, and a few additional characters that enhance its phonetic richness. Here, we explore the letters of the German alphabet, their pronunciation, and the unique characters that set German apart from other languages. Understanding the German alphabet is essential for anyone looking to learn the language or delve into its literature and culture.

The Letters of the German Alphabet

The German alphabet includes the following 26 letters:

A, B, C, D, E, F, G, H, I, J, K, L, M, N, O, P, Q, R, S, T, U, V, W, X, Y, Z

Each letter has a specific pronunciation, which may differ from its English counterpart.

Here's a brief overview of how to pronounce each letter:

A - pronounced like "ah"

B - pronounced like "beh"

C - pronounced like "tseh"

D - pronounced like "deh"

E - pronounced like "eh"

F - pronounced like "eff"

G - pronounced like "geh"

H - pronounced like "hah"

I - pronounced like "ee"

J - pronounced like "yot"

K - pronounced like "kah"

L - pronounced like "ell"

M - pronounced like "emm"

N - pronounced like "enn"

O - pronounced like "oh"

P - pronounced like "peh"

Q - pronounced like "koo"

R - pronounced like "ehr"

S - pronounced like "ess"

T - pronounced like "teh"

U - pronounced like "oo"

V - pronounced like "fau"

W - pronounced like "veh"

X - pronounced like "iks"

Y - pronounced like "üpsilon"

Z - pronounced like "tset"

Special Characters

In addition to the standard letters, the German alphabet includes three special characters known as umlauts and the sharp S:

Ä - pronounced like "eh"

Ö - pronounced like "oe"

Ü - pronounced like "ue"

ß - known as "Eszett" or "sharp S," pronounced like "ss"

These characters modify the pronunciation of the base vowels and are crucial for proper spelling and pronunciation in German.

The German alphabet is a vital language component, providing the foundation for reading, writing, and communication. By familiarizing oneself with the letters and pronunciations, learners can enhance their understanding of German and engage more deeply with its culture and literature. Whether you are a beginner or looking to refine your skills, mastering the German alphabet is essential to your language journey.

Multiple-Choice Questions on The German Alphabet

1. How many letters are there in the German alphabet?

a) 24

b) 25

c) 26

d) 30

Answer: c) 26

2. What is the German letter "J" correct pronunciation?

a) Jot

b) Yot

c) Jet

d) Gee

Answer: b) Yot

3. Which of the following is NOT a letter in the German alphabet?

a) Q

b) ß

c) X

d) Ñ

Answer: d) Ñ

4. What is the German pronunciation of the letter "W"?

a) Double-u

b) Veh

c) Way

d) Wah

Answer: b) Veh

5. Which special character is also known as "Eszett" or "sharp S"?

a) Ü

b) ß

c) Ö

d) Ä

Answer: b) ß

6. How is the German letter "C" pronounced?

a) Tseh

b) Seh

c) Kuh

d) Ess

Answer: a) Tseh

7. What is the correct pronunciation of "R" in German?

a) Air

b) Ehr

c) Err

d) Rah

Answer: b) Ehr

8. Which of the following German vowels has an umlaut?

a) A

b) O

c) U

d) All of the above

Answer: d) All of the above

9. Which of the following German letters is pronounced like "f"?

a) P

b) V

c) X

d) T

Answer: b) V

10. What does the umlaut in "Ü" change in pronunciation?

a) It makes the sound deeper

b) It gives a more rounded vowel sound

c) It turns into a nasal sound

d) It has no effect

Answer: b) It gives a more rounded vowel sound

11. Which German letter sounds like the English "ts" sound?

a) T

b) S

c) Z

d) C

Answer: c) Z

12. How do you pronounce the German letter "O"?

a) Ah

b) Oh

c) Ow

d) Uh

Answer: b) Oh

13. Which of the following is a special character in German?

a) È

b) Ä

c) Ň

d) Ç

Answer: b) Ä

14. Which letter in German is pronounced like "iks"?

a) Y

b) X

c) V

d) Q

Answer: b) X

15. Which special letters modifies the vowel "A"?

a) Ä

b) Ö

c) Ü

d) ß

Answer: a) Ä

16. Which German letter is pronounced as "koo"?

a) P

b) Q

c) R

d) S

Answer: b) Q

17. What is the German pronunciation of "E"?

a) Eh

b) Ee

c) Ah

d) Uh

Answer: a) Eh

18. Which German letter has a pronunciation similar to "tset"?

a) S

b) C

c) Z

d) T

Answer: c) Z

19. Which of the following letters is NOT pronounced the same as in English?

a) F

b) B

c) V

d) M

Answer: c) V

20. How do you pronounce the German letter "I"?

a) Eh

b) Ee

c) Ai

d) Uh

Answer: b) Ee

21. What is the primary function of umlauts in the German alphabet?

a) To create new letters

b) To change the pronunciation of vowels

c) To add emphasis to words

d) To replace consonants

Answer: b) To change the pronunciation of vowels

22. How do you pronounce the German letter "K"?

a) Kah

b) Kuh

c) Kih

d) Key

Answer: a) Kah

23. Which of the following letters sounds like "fau" in German?

a) F

b) V

c) W

d) Z

Answer: b) V

24. How do you pronounce the German letter "D"?

a) Deh

b) Dah

c) Dee

d) Doe

Answer: a) Deh

25. Which German letter is pronounced "ell"?

a) L

b) J

c) P

d) Q

Answer: a) L

ᗡᗡᗡ

TWO

NUMBERS AND COUNTING

Numbers and Counting in German

Here, we have an overview of numbers and counting in German. It covers basic numbers, how to form more significant numbers and some useful phrases related to counting. Understanding these concepts is essential for anyone learning German, as numbers are fundamental to everyday communication.

Basic Numbers

Here are the basic numbers from 0 to 10 in German:

Number	German
0	null
1	eins
2	zwei
3	drei

| 4 | *vier* |

| 5 | *fünf* |

| 6 | *sechs* |

| 7 | *sieben* |

| 8 | *acht* |

| 9 | *neun* |

| 10 | *zehn* |

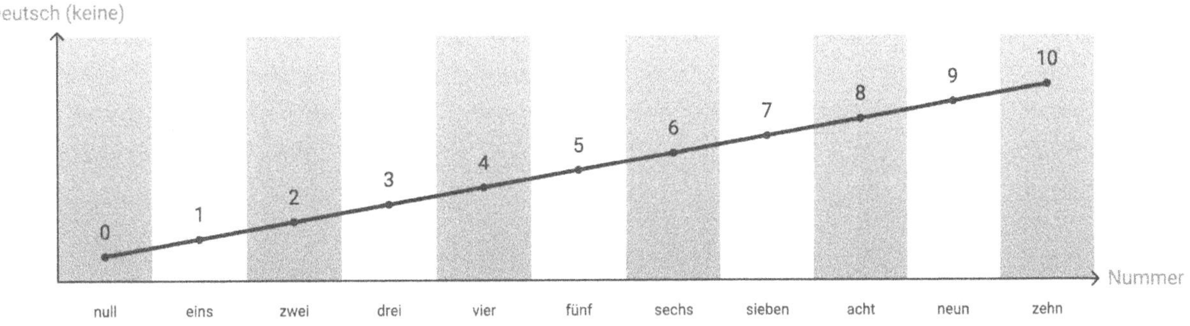

Grundzahlen von 0 bis 10 auf Deutsch

Numbers 11 to 20

The numbers from 11 to 20 in German are formed with a combination of the basic numbers and specific suffixes:

| Number | German |

|--------|----------|

| 11 | elf |

| 12 | zwölf |

| 13 | dreizehn |

| 14 | vierzehn |

| 15 | fünfzehn |

| 16 | sechzehn |

| 17 | siebzehn |

| 18 | achtzehn |

| 19 | neunzehn |

| 20 | zwanzig |

Counting Beyond 20

To count beyond 20, German combines the tens and the units. Here's how it works:

21: einundzwanzig (one and twenty)

22: zweiundzwanzig (two and twenty)

30: dreißig (thirty)

31: einunddreißig (one and thirty)

40: vierzig (forty)

50: fünfzig (fifty)

60: sechzig (sixty)

70: siebzig (seventy)

80: achtzig (eighty)

90: neunzig (ninety)

100: hundert (hundred)

Larger Numbers

For larger numbers, German follows a similar pattern:

101: einhunderteins (one hundred one)

200: zweihundert (two hundred)

1,000: tausend (thousand)

1,000,000: eine Million (one million)

Useful Phrases

Here are some useful phrases related to counting in German:

Wie viel kostet das? (How much does that cost?)

Ich habe zwei Äpfel. (I have two apples.)

Zähle bis zehn! (Count to ten!)

Es gibt fünf Bücher. (There are five books.)

Understanding numbers and counting in German is crucial for effective communication. With practice, you will become more comfortable using numbers in everyday conversations.

Multiple-Choice Questions on Numbers and Counting in German

1. What is the German word for "zero"?
a) eins
b) null
c) zehn
d) sieben
Answer: b) null
    2. How do you say "five" in German?
a) vier
b) fünf
c) sechs
d) acht

Answer: b) fünf

3. What is the German word for "ten"?

a) zehn

b) zwanzig

c) sechzehn

d) hundert

Answer: a) zehn

4. How do you say "twelve" in German?

a) zwanzig

b) fünfzehn

c) zwölf

d) dreizehn

Answer: c) zwölf

5. What is the German word for "nineteen"?

a) neunzig

b) neunzehn

c) siebzehn

d) vierzehn

Answer: b) neunzehn

6. How do you say "twenty" in German?

a) siebzig

b) zwanzig

c) dreißig

d) vierzig

Answer: b) zwanzig

7. What is "thirty" in German?

a) dreißig

b) sechzig

c) fünfzig

d) vierzig

Answer: a) dreißig

8. What is the correct way to say "forty" in German?

a) siebzig

b) zwanzig

c) vierzig

d) achtzig

Answer: c) vierzig

9. How do you say "seventy" in German?

a) sieben

b) siebzig

c) siebzehn

d) sechzig

Answer: b) siebzig

10. What is the German word for "one hundred"?

a) tausend

b) eine Million

c) hundert

d) neunzig

Answer: c) hundert

11. How do you say "one thousand" in German?

a) hundert

b) tausend

c) eine Million

d) zehn

Answer: b) tausend

12. What is the German word for "one million"?

a) tausend

b) hundert

c) eine Million

d) fünfzig

Answer: c) eine Million

13. How do you say "21" in German?

a) zwanzigeins

b) einundzwanzig

c) zwanzigein

d) zwanzigeinen

Answer: b) einundzwanzig

14. What is the correct translation for "35" in German?

a) fünfunddreißig

b) dreiundvierzig

c) vierunddreißig

d) sechunddreißig

Answer: a) fünfunddreißig

15. How do you say "47" in German?

a) siebzehn

b) siebenundvierzig

c) siebenunddreißig

d) vierzehn

Answer: b) siebenundvierzig

16. What is "52" in German?

a) fünfundzwanzig

b) fünfzig

c) zweiundfünfzig

d) fünfundvierzig

Answer: c) zweiundfünfzig

17. How do you say "99" in German?

a) neunundneunzig

b) neunzehn

c) neunzig

d) achtundneunzig

Answer: a) neunundneunzig

18. What does "Ich habe zwei Äpfel" mean?

a) I have two apples

b) I like apples

c) I eat apples

d) I need apples

Answer: a) I have two apples

19. What is the German translation for "How much does that cost?"

a) Was ist das?

b) Wie viel kostet das?

c) Wie heißt du?

d) Wo ist das?

Answer: b) Wie viel kostet das?

20. How do you say "Count to ten!" in German?

a) Zähle bis zehn!

b) Gehe nach zehn!

c) Warte zehn Minuten!

d) Spreche zehn Mal!

Answer: a) Zähle bis zehn!

21. What is "Es gibt fünf Bücher" in English?

a) There are five books

b) I have five books

c) We need five books

d) Five books are here

Answer: a) There are five books

22. What is the German word for "sixty"?

a) sechzig

b) sechzehn

c) siebzig

d) sechs

Answer: a) sechzig

23. How do you say "88" in German?

a) achtundachtzig

b) achtzig

c) neunzig

d) achtundzwanzig

Answer: a) achtundachtzig

24. How is "102" written in German?

a) hundertzwei

b) einhundertzwei

c) hundertzweiundzwanzig

d) zweiundhundert

Answer: b) einhundertzwei

25. Which of the following is correct for "250" in German?

a) zweihundertfünfzig

b) zweihundertundfünfzig

c) zwei hundert fünfzig

d) fünfzigzweihundert

Answer: a) zweihundertfünfzig

ppp

THREE
Common Phrases in German

Here's a list of common German phrases useful for everyday conversations.

These phrases cover greetings, questions, expressions, and more:

Greetings and Introductions

Hallo - Hello

Guten Morgen - Good morning

Guten Tag - Good afternoon / Good day

Guten Abend - Good evening

Gute Nacht - Good night

Wie geht es dir? - How are you? (informal)

Wie geht es Ihnen? - How are you? (formal)

Mir geht es gut, danke. - I'm fine, thank you.

Und dir? - And you? (informal)

Und Ihnen? - And you? (formal)

Basic Questions

Wie heißt du? - What's your name? (informal)

Wie heißen Sie? - What's your name? (formal)

Ich heiße... - My name is...

Woher kommst du? - Where are you from? (informal)

Woher kommen Sie? - Where are you from? (formal)

Ich komme aus... - I'm from...

Wie alt bist du? - How old are you? (informal)

Wie alt sind Sie? - How old are you? (formal)

Ich bin ... Jahre alt. - I'm ... years old.

Sprechen Sie Englisch? - Do you speak English?

Polite Expressions

Bitte - Please / You're welcome

Danke - Thank you

Vielen Dank - Thank you very much

Gern geschehen - You're welcome

Entschuldigung - Excuse me / Sorry

Es tut mir leid - I'm sorry

Kein Problem - No problem

Natürlich - Of course

Können Sie mir helfen? - Can you help me?

Ich verstehe nicht - I don't understand

Common Phrases for Daily Life

Wie spät ist es? - What time is it?

Ich habe Hunger. - I'm hungry.

Ich habe Durst. - I'm thirsty.

Ich bin müde. - I'm tired.

Wo ist die Toilette? - Where is the bathroom?

Ich brauche Hilfe. - I need help.

Ich weiß nicht. - I don't know.

Ich habe eine Frage. - I have a question.

Es ist heiß. - It's hot.

Es ist kalt. - It's cold.

Shopping and Dining

Wie viel kostet das? - How much does it cost?

Ich möchte... - I would like...

Haben Sie...? - Do you have...?

Die Rechnung, bitte. - The bill, please.

Was empfehlen Sie? - What do you recommend?

Es schmeckt gut. - It tastes good.

Ich bin Vegetarier/Vegetarierin. - I'm vegetarian.

Wo ist der Markt? - Where is the market?

Akzeptieren Sie Karten? - Do you accept cards?

Das ist zu teuer. - It's too expensive.

Travel and Directions

Wo ist der Bahnhof? - Where is the train station?

Wie komme ich zu...? - How do I get to...?

Ich habe mich verlaufen. - I'm lost.

Rechts - To the right

Links - To the left

Geradeaus - Straight ahead

Ist es weit? - Is it far?

Ist es nah? - Is it nearby?

Wo kann ich ein Taxi finden? - Where can I find a taxi?

Ich brauche eine Karte. - I need a map.

Feelings and Opinions

Ich bin glücklich. - I'm happy.

Ich bin traurig. - I'm sad.

Ich bin wütend. - I'm angry.

Das gefällt mir. - I like it.

Das gefällt mir nicht. - I don't like it.

Es ist schön. - It's beautiful.

Es ist hässlich. - It's ugly.

Es ist interessant. - It's interesting.

Es ist langweilig. - It's boring.

Ich stimme zu. - I agree.

At Home

Wo ist der Schlüssel? - Where is the key?

Ich gehe nach Hause. - I'm going home.

Ich gehe schlafen. - I'm going to sleep.

Was gibt es zu essen? - What's for dinner?

Pass auf! - Be careful!

Räum dein Zimmer auf. - Clean your room.

Ich gehe duschen. - I'm going to take a shower.

Mach das Licht an. - Turn on the light.

Mach den Fernseher aus. - Turn off the TV.

Ich gehe einkaufen. - I'm going shopping.

Work and School

Ich arbeite. *- I'm working.*

Ich bin spät dran. - I'm late.

Ich habe einen Termin. - I have an appointment.

Was ist dein Beruf? - What is your job?

Ich bin Student/Studentin. - I'm a student.

Ich habe morgen eine Prüfung. - I have an exam tomorrow.

Es ist schwierig. - It's difficult.

Es ist einfach. - It's easy.

Ich muss lernen. - I have to study.

Ich gehe ins Büro. - I'm going to the office.

Health and Emergencies

Ich habe Kopfschmerzen. - I have a headache.

Ich brauche einen Arzt. - I need a doctor.

Rufen Sie einen Krankenwagen! - Call an ambulance!

Wo ist das Krankenhaus? - Where is the hospital?

Ich bin krank. - I'm sick.

Hilfe! - Help!

Ich bin allergisch gegen... - I'm allergic to...

Wo ist die Apotheke? - Where is the pharmacy?

Ich habe meinen Pass verloren. - I lost my passport.

Notfall! - Emergency!

These phrases are a great starting point for building confidence in German.

Multiple-Choice Questions on Common German Phrases

1. How do you say "Good morning" in German?
a) Guten Abend
b) Guten Morgen
c) Gute Nacht
d) Hallo
Answer: b) Guten Morgen
2. What is the German phrase for "How are you?" (informal)?
a) Wie heißen Sie?
b) Wie alt sind Sie?
c) Wie geht es dir?
d) Woher kommst du?
Answer: c) Wie geht es dir?
3. How do you say "Good night" in German?
a) Gute Nacht
b) Guten Abend
c) Guten Tag
d) Hallo
Answer: a) Gute Nacht
4. What is the German phrase for "My name is..."?
a) Ich bin...
b) Ich heiße...

c) Woher kommst du?

d) Ich habe...

Answer: b) Ich heiße...

    5. How do you ask "Where are you from?" in German? (formal)

a) Woher kommst du?

b) Woher kommen Sie?

c) Wie heißen Sie?

d) Wo ist das?

Answer: b) Woher kommen Sie?

    6. How do you say "Thank you very much" in German?

a) Bitte

b) Danke

c) Vielen Dank

d) Es tut mir leid

Answer: c) Vielen Dank

    7. Which phrase means "I don't understand"?

a) Ich habe eine Frage

b) Ich verstehe nicht

c) Ich stimme zu

d) Ich gehe einkaufen

Answer: b) Ich verstehe nicht

    8. How do you say "Where is the bathroom?" in German?

a) Wo ist der Markt?

b) Wo ist die Toilette?

c) Wie viel kostet das?

d) Wo kann ich ein Taxi finden?

Answer: b) Wo ist die Toilette?

    9. What is the German phrase for "I'm hungry"?

a) Ich habe Hunger

b) Ich habe Durst

c) Ich bin müde

d) Ich brauche Hilfe

Answer: a) Ich habe Hunger

    10. What does "Wie viel kostet das?" mean?

a) Where is the train station?

b) How much does it cost?

c) What is your name?

d) Do you speak English?

Answer: b) How much does it cost?

11. What is "I'm vegetarian" in German?

a) Ich habe Hunger

b) Ich bin Vegetarier/Vegetarierin

c) Ich bin müde

d) Ich brauche eine Karte

Answer: b) Ich bin Vegetarier/Vegetarierin

12. How do you ask "Where is the train station?" in German?

a) Wo ist der Bahnhof?

b) Wo kann ich ein Taxi finden?

c) Ist es weit?

d) Wo ist der Markt?

Answer: a) Wo ist der Bahnhof?

13. What does "Rechts" mean?

a) Left

b) Straight ahead

c) Right

d) Far

Answer: c) Right

14. How do you say "I'm happy" in German?

a) Ich bin traurig

b) Ich bin wütend

c) Ich bin glücklich

d) Ich bin krank

Answer: c) Ich bin glücklich

15. What does "Das gefällt mir nicht" mean?

a) I like it

b) I don't like it

c) It is boring

d) It is beautiful

Answer: b) I don't like it

16. What does "Ich gehe nach Hause" mean?

a) I'm going to sleep

b) I'm going home

c) I'm working

d) I need a doctor

Answer: b) I'm going home

17. Which phrase means "Turn on the light"?

a) Mach das Licht an

b) Mach den Fernseher aus

c) Pass auf!

d) Räum dein Zimmer auf

Answer: a) Mach das Licht an

18. How do you say "I'm working" in German?

a) Ich arbeite

b) Ich muss lernen

c) Ich bin Student

d) Ich gehe schlafen

Answer: a) Ich arbeite

19. What does "Ich habe morgen eine Prüfung" mean?

a) I have an exam tomorrow

b) I have an appointment

c) I am going to the office

d) I have a question

Answer: a) I have an exam tomorrow

20. How do you say "Call an ambulance!" in German?

a) Wo ist das Krankenhaus?

b) Rufen Sie einen Krankenwagen!

c) Ich brauche einen Arzt

d) Ich bin krank

Answer: b) Rufen Sie einen Krankenwagen!

21. What does "Hilfe!" mean?

a) Hello

b) Help!

c) Goodbye

d) Thank you

Answer: b) Help!

22. How do you say "I lost my passport" in German?

a) Ich brauche einen Arzt

b) Ich habe meinen Pass verloren

c) Wo ist die Apotheke?

d) Ich stimme zu

Answer: b) Ich habe meinen Pass verloren

23. What is "I need help" in German?

a) Ich brauche Hilfe

b) Ich bin krank

c) Ich habe Hunger

d) Ich verstehe nicht

Answer: a) Ich brauche Hilfe

24. How do you say "Where can I find a taxi?" in German?

a) Wo kann ich ein Taxi finden?

b) Wie komme ich zu...?

c) Ich habe mich verlaufen

d) Ich brauche eine Karte

Answer: a) Wo kann ich ein Taxi finden?

25. What does "Ich gehe duschen" mean?

a) I am going shopping

b) I am taking a shower

c) I am hungry

d) I am working

Answer: b) I am taking a shower

▷▷▷

FOUR
ASKING FOR DIRECTIONS

Whether you are travelling to Germany or simply want to practice your language skills, knowing how to ask for directions can be incredibly useful.

Here are a few key expressions, common questions, and helpful tips for navigating German-speaking areas.

Basic Phrases

Here are some fundamental phrases to get you started:

Entschuldigung, wo ist...? (Excuse me, where is...?)

Könnten Sie mir bitte helfen? (Could you please help me?)

Ich suche... (I am looking for...)

Wie komme ich zu...? (How do I get to...?)

Ist es weit von hier? (Is it far from here?)

Common Questions

When asking for directions, you might want to use the following questions:

Gibt es eine U-Bahn-Station in der Nähe? (Is there a subway station nearby?)

Wie lange dauert es, um dorthin zu gelangen? (How long does it take to get there?)

Welcher Weg führt zu...? (Which way leads to...?)

Könnte ich eine Karte bekommen? (Could I get a map?)

Vocabulary for Directions

Familiarize yourself with these directional terms:

links (left)

rechts (right)

geradeaus (straight ahead)

um die Ecke (around the corner)

überqueren (to cross)

Example Dialogues

Here are a couple of example dialogues to illustrate how to ask for directions:

Dialogue 1

Tourist: Entschuldigung, wo ist die nächste U-Bahn-Station?

Local: Gehen Sie geradeaus und dann nach links. Die U-Bahn-Station ist auf der rechten Seite.

Dialogue 2

Tourist: Ich suche das Museum. Wie komme ich dorthin?

Local: Gehen Sie geradeaus, überqueren Sie die Straße, und das Museum ist auf der linken Seite.

Tips for Asking for Directions

Be Polite: Always start with "Entschuldigung" (Excuse me) to show respect.

Listen Carefully: Pay attention to the directions, and don't hesitate to ask for clarification if needed.

Practice Pronunciation: Try to practice the phrases out loud to improve your pronunciation.

Use Gestures: Sometimes, using hand gestures can help convey your message more clearly.

Asking for directions in German can enhance your travel experience and help you connect with locals. By using the phrases and vocabulary provided in this document, you will be better equipped to navigate your way through German-speaking regions.

Remember to practice regularly, and don't be afraid to engage with others in the language!

Multiple-Choice Questions on Asking for Directions in German

1. How do you say "Excuse me, where is...?" in German?
a) Ich suche...
b) Entschuldigung, wo ist...?
c) Wie komme ich zu...?
d) Könnte ich eine Karte bekommen?
Answer: b) Entschuldigung, wo ist...?

2. Which phrase means "Could you please help me?"
a) Könnten Sie mir bitte helfen?
b) Ist es weit von hier?
c) Gibt es eine U-Bahn-Station in der Nähe?
d) Welcher Weg führt zu...?
Answer: a) Könnten Sie mir bitte helfen?

3. How do you say "I am looking for..." in German?
a) Ich gehe geradeaus
b) Ich suche...
c) Ich brauche eine Karte
d) Ich habe mich verlaufen
Answer: b) Ich suche...

4. What does "Wie komme ich zu...?" mean?
a) How do I get to...?
b) Where is...?
c) How long does it take?
d) Is it far?
Answer: a) How do I get to...?

5. Which of the following means "Is there a subway station nearby?"
a) Wo ist der Bahnhof?
b) Gibt es eine U-Bahn-Station in der Nähe?
c) Ich suche die Bushaltestelle
d) Wo kann ich ein Taxi finden?
Answer: b) Gibt es eine U-Bahn-Station in der Nähe?

6. How do you ask "How long does it take to get there?" in German?

a) Wie lange dauert es, um dorthin zu gelangen?

b) Wo ist die nächste U-Bahn-Station?

c) Ich suche das Museum

d) Wie spät ist es?

Answer: a) Wie lange dauert es, um dorthin zu gelangen?

7. What does "Welcher Weg führt zu...?" mean?

a) Which way leads to...?

b) Where is...?

c) How far is it?

d) How do I get there?

Answer: a) Which way leads to...?

8. Which phrase means "Could I get a map?"

a) Ich habe Hunger

b) Könnte ich eine Karte bekommen?

c) Wo ist die Toilette?

d) Ich brauche eine U-Bahn-Station

Answer: b) Könnte ich eine Karte bekommen?

9. What is the German word for "left"?

a) links

b) rechts

c) geradeaus

d) um die Ecke

Answer: a) links

10. How do you say "right" in German?

a) links

b) geradeaus

c) rechts

d) überqueren

Answer: c) rechts

11. What does "geradeaus" mean?

a) Around the corner

b) Straight ahead

c) To cross

d) Left

Answer: b) Straight ahead

12. Which phrase means "around the corner"?

a) links

b) rechts

c) um die Ecke

d) überqueren

Answer: c) um die Ecke

13. What does "überqueren" mean in English?

a) To cross

b) To walk

c) To go left

d) To wait

Answer: a) To cross

14. How do you say "Go straight ahead and then turn left" in German?

a) Gehen Sie geradeaus und dann nach links

b) Gehen Sie um die Ecke und dann nach rechts

c) Gehen Sie über die Brücke und dann nach rechts

d) Gehen Sie links und dann nach rechts

Answer: a) Gehen Sie geradeaus und dann nach links

15. Which of these is a polite way to ask for directions?

a) Ich brauche Hilfe!

b) Entschuldigung, können Sie mir helfen?

c) Wo ist das?

d) Ich weiß nicht

Answer: b) Entschuldigung, können Sie mir helfen?

16. What is a good way to clarify if you don't understand the directions?

a) Ich verstehe nicht

b) Ist es weit von hier?

c) Wo ist der Bahnhof?

d) Ich stimme zu

Answer: a) Ich verstehe nicht

17. What does "Wo ist die nächste U-Bahn-Station?" mean?

a) Where is the next subway station?

b) Where is the next bus stop?

c) How much does a ticket cost?

d) How do I buy a subway ticket?

Answer: a) Where is the next subway station?

18. How do you say "The museum is on the left side" in German?

a) Das Museum ist auf der linken Seite

b) Das Museum ist auf der rechten Seite

c) Das Museum ist um die Ecke

d) Das Museum ist gegenüber

Answer: a) Das Museum ist auf der linken Seite

19. What is the best way to ask for a map?

a) Ich brauche ein Ticket

b) Ich brauche eine Karte

c) Ich brauche eine Uhr

d) Ich brauche ein Taxi

Answer: b) Ich brauche eine Karte

20. What does "Ist es weit von hier?" mean?

a) Is it far from here?

b) Where is it?

c) Can I get a ticket?

d) How do I get there?

Answer: a) Is it far from here?

21. What phrase would help if you are lost?

a) Ich habe mich verlaufen

b) Ich habe eine Frage

c) Ich habe Hunger

d) Ich brauche ein Taxi

Answer: a) Ich habe mich verlaufen

22. What does "Rechts abbiegen" mean?

a) Turn left

b) Turn right

c) Go straight

d) Cross the street

Answer: b) Turn right

23. Which phrase means "Cross the street"?

a) Überqueren Sie die Straße

b) Gehen Sie links

c) Gehen Sie geradeaus

d) Um die Ecke gehen

Answer: a) Überqueren Sie die Straße

24. What does "Der Bahnhof ist geradeaus" mean?

a) The train station is straight ahead

b) The bus station is on the left

c) The airport is far away

d) The taxi stand is around the corner

Answer: a) The train station is straight ahead

25. What is a good tip for asking for directions?

a) Be polite and start with "Entschuldigung"

b) Always speak English

c) Ignore gestures and body language

d) Don't practice pronunciation

Answer: a) Be polite and start with "Entschuldigung"

ᐅᐅᐅ

FIVE
AT A RESTAURANT

Greetings and Asking for a Table

1. Arriving at the Restaurant

Hallo, wir hätten gern einen Tisch für ... Personen.

Hello, we'd like a table for ... people.

Haben Sie eine Reservierung?

Do you have a reservation?

Ja, unter dem Namen ...

Yes, under the name ...

Nein, haben wir nicht.

No, we don't.

Können wir draußen sitzen?

Can we sit outside?

Guten Tag! – Good day!

Haben Sie einen Tisch für zwei/drei/vier Personen? – Do you have a table for two/three/four people?

Ich habe eine Reservierung auf den Namen ... – I have a reservation under the name ...

Können wir bitte die Speisekarte sehen? – Can we see the menu, please?

Asking for Recommendations

Was empfehlen Sie?

What do you recommend?

Was ist die Spezialität des Hauses?

What's the house's speciality?

Gibt es vegetarische Gerichte?

Do you have vegetarian dishes?

Ist das scharf?

Is this spicy?

Was ist in diesem Gericht enthalten?

What's in this dish?

Ordering Food and Drinks

Ich hätte gern … – I would like …

Ich nehme … – I'll take …

Was können Sie empfehlen? – What can you recommend?

Gibt es vegetarische Gerichte? – Are there vegetarian dishes?

Ich bin allergisch gegen ... – I am allergic to ...

Könnte ich bitte ein Glas Wasser haben? – Could I have a glass of water, please?

Ich hätte gern...

I would like...

Ich nehme...

I'll take...

Können wir die Speisekarte sehen?

Can we see the menu?

Ich möchte das gleiche wie er/sie.

I'll have the same as him/her.

Können Sie das ohne ... machen?

Can you make that without ...?

Ich bin allergisch gegen...

I'm allergic to...

Können wir noch etwas Zeit haben?

Can we have a little more time?

Können wir etwas zu trinken bestellen?

Can we order something to drink?

Ein Glas Wasser, bitte.

A glass of water, please.

Haben Sie deutsche Weine?

Do you have German wines?

Ich hätte gern eine Tasse Kaffee.

I'd like a cup of coffee.

Ein Bier, bitte.

A beer, please.

Asking About the Menu

Was ist das Tagesgericht? – What is the daily special?

Gibt es eine Kinderkarte? – Is there a children's menu?

Ist das scharf? – Is this spicy?

Wie lange dauert es? – How long will it take?

During the Meal

Das schmeckt sehr gut! – This tastes very good!

Könnte ich noch etwas Brot haben? – Could I have some more bread?

Könnten wir bitte noch eine Runde Getränke bestellen? – Could we order another round of drinks, please?

Das schmeckt ausgezeichnet!

This tastes excellent!

Können wir noch Brot bekommen?

Can we get more bread?

Könnten Sie mir bitte ... bringen?

Could you please bring me ...?

Entschuldigung, das ist nicht, was ich bestellt habe.

Excuse me, this isn't what I ordered.

Können wir die Rechnung haben?

Can we have the bill?

Asking for the Bill and Payment

Die Rechnung, bitte. – The bill, please.

Kann ich mit Karte bezahlen? – Can I pay by card?

Stimmt so. – Keep the change.

War alles in Ordnung? – Was everything okay?

Zusammen oder getrennt? Together or separate?

Kann ich mit Karte zahlen? Can I pay with a card?

Nehmen Sie Kreditkarten? Do you accept credit cards?

Stimmt so. Keep the change.

Können Sie uns die Rechnung bringen? Can you bring us the bill?

Compliments and Complaints

Das Essen war hervorragend! The food was excellent!

Danke für den tollen Service! Thank you for the great service!

Entschuldigung, das ist kalt. Excuse me, this is cold.

Könnten Sie das bitte umtauschen? Could you please replace this?

Useful Vocabulary

die Speisekarte - the menu

die Vorspeise - the appetizer

das Hauptgericht - the main course

die Nachspeise - the dessert

die Rechnung - the bill

der Kellner / die Kellnerin - the waiter / waitress

das Trinkgeld - the tip

vegetarisch - vegetarian

vegan - vegan

scharf - spicy

süß - sweet

salzig - salty

Example Conversation

Kellner: Guten Abend, haben Sie eine Reservierung? [Good evening, do you have a reservation?]
Gast: Guten Abend, ja, unter dem Namen Müller. [Good evening, yes, under the name Müller.]

Kellner: Bitte folgen Sie mir. Hier ist Ihre Speisekarte. [Please follow me. Here is your menu.]
Gast: Danke. Was empfehlen Sie? [Thank you. What do you recommend?]
Kellner: Unser Schweinebraten ist sehr beliebt. [Our roast pork is very popular.]
Gast: Gut, ich nehme den Schweinebraten. Und ein Glas Rotwein, bitte. [Okay, I'll have the roast pork. And a glass of red wine, please.]
Kellner: Sehr gut. Möchten Sie eine Vorspeise? [Very good. Would you like an appetizer?]
Gast: Ja, ich hätte gern die Suppe. [Yes, I would like the soup.]
Kellner: Kommt sofort. [Come immediately.]

With these phrases, you can confidently navigate a restaurant experience in German.

Multiple-Choice Questions on Restaurant Conversations in German

1. How do you say, "Do you have a reservation?" in German?
a) Haben Sie einen Tisch?
b) Haben Sie eine Speisekarte?
c) Haben Sie eine Reservierung?
d) Haben Sie ein Menü?
Answer: c) Haben Sie eine Reservierung?

2. What would you say if you didn't have a reservation?
a) Ja, unter dem Namen Müller.
b) Nein, haben wir nicht.
c) Ich hätte gern eine Speisekarte.
d) Ich nehme eine Vorspeise.
Answer: b) Nein, haben wir nicht.

3. How do you ask if you can sit outside?
a) Können wir die Speisekarte sehen?
b) Können wir draußen sitzen?
c) Können wir etwas zu trinken bestellen?
d) Können wir ein Glas Wasser haben?
Answer: b) Können wir draußen sitzen?

4. Which phrase means "Can we see the menu, please?"

a) Haben Sie eine Reservierung?

b) Können wir die Rechnung haben?

c) Können wir bitte die Speisekarte sehen?

d) Können wir draußen sitzen?

Answer: c) Können wir bitte die Speisekarte sehen?

5. What does "Ich habe eine Reservierung auf den Namen ..." mean?

a) I have a reservation under the name ...

b) I would like to order ...

c) I want a table outside.

d) I would like a drink.

Answer: a) I have a reservation under the name ...

6. How do you ask "What do you recommend?" in German?

a) Was ist das Tagesgericht?

b) Was empfehlen Sie?

c) Ist das scharf?

d) Was kostet das?

Answer: b) Was empfehlen Sie?

7. Which question asks about the restaurant's specialty?

a) Gibt es vegetarische Gerichte?

b) Was ist die Spezialität des Hauses?

c) Können wir die Rechnung haben?

d) Ist das salzig?

Answer: b) Was ist die Spezialität des Hauses?

8. How do you ask if a dish is spicy?

a) Gibt es vegetarische Gerichte?

b) Was ist das Tagesgericht?

c) Ist das scharf?

d) Können wir noch etwas Brot bekommen?

Answer: c) Ist das scharf?

9. What does "Gibt es vegetarische Gerichte?" mean?

a) Do you have vegetarian dishes?

b) What is the house specialty?

c) Can we get more bread?

d) Is this spicy?

Answer: a) Do you have vegetarian dishes?

    10. Which phrase means "What is in this dish?"

a) Was ist die Spezialität des Hauses?

b) Was ist in diesem Gericht enthalten?

c) Wie lange dauert es?

d) Ist das süß?

Answer: b) Was ist in diesem Gericht enthalten?

    11. How do you say "I would like ..." in German?

a) Ich hätte gern ...

b) Ich nehme ...

c) Ich bin allergisch gegen ...

d) Ich habe eine Reservierung ...

Answer: a) Ich hätte gern ...

    12. What does "Ich nehme ..." mean?

a) I am allergic to ...

b) I'll take ...

c) I have a reservation ...

d) Can we order something to drink?

Answer: b) I'll take ...

    13. How do you ask for a glass of water?

a) Ein Glas Wasser, bitte.

b) Können wir draußen sitzen?

c) Haben Sie deutsche Weine?

d) Ich hätte gern eine Tasse Kaffee.

Answer: a) Ein Glas Wasser, bitte.

    14. What would you say if you are allergic to something?

a) Ich nehme das Tagesgericht.

b) Ich bin allergisch gegen ...

c) Ich hätte gern eine Speisekarte.

d) Können wir draußen sitzen?

Answer: b) Ich bin allergisch gegen ...

    15. Which phrase means "Can we have a little more time?"

a) Können wir die Rechnung haben?

b) Können wir noch etwas Zeit haben?

c) Können wir noch Brot bekommen?

d) Können Sie uns die Rechnung bringen?

Answer: b) Können wir noch etwas Zeit haben?

16. How do you say, "This tastes very good!" in German?

a) Das schmeckt sehr gut!

b) Ist das süß?

c) Können wir die Rechnung haben?

d) Ich hätte gern eine Speisekarte.

Answer: a) Das schmeckt sehr gut!

17. How do you ask for more bread?

a) Können wir noch Brot bekommen?

b) Ich hätte gern eine Tasse Kaffee.

c) Können Sie das ohne ... machen?

d) Haben Sie vegetarische Gerichte?

Answer: a) Können wir noch Brot bekommen?

18. How do you politely ask for something to be brought to you?

a) Entschuldigung, das ist nicht, was ich bestellt habe.

b) Können wir die Rechnung haben?

c) Könnten Sie mir bitte ... bringen?

d) Ich nehme ein Bier.

Answer: c) Könnten Sie mir bitte ... bringen?

19. How do you ask for the bill?

a) Können wir die Rechnung haben?

b) Haben Sie deutsche Weine?

c) Ich nehme das Tagesgericht.

d) Was empfehlen Sie?

Answer: a) Können wir die Rechnung haben?

20. How do you ask if you can pay by card?

a) Kann ich mit Karte bezahlen?

b) Ich hätte gern ein Glas Wasser.

c) Haben Sie eine Reservierung?

d) Ist das scharf?

Answer: a) Kann ich mit Karte bezahlen?

21. What does "Stimmt so." mean?

a) Keep the change.

b) The food was cold.

c) This is not what I ordered.

d) Can we have the menu?

Answer: a) Keep the change.

22. How do you say "The food was excellent!" in German?

a) Das Essen war hervorragend!

b) Können wir die Rechnung haben?

c) Ich nehme ein Glas Wasser.

d) Haben Sie eine Reservierung?

Answer: a) Das Essen war hervorragend!

23. Which phrase means "Excuse me, this is cold."?

a) Danke für den tollen Service!

b) Entschuldigung, das ist kalt.

c) Können wir die Rechnung haben?

d) Ist das scharf?

Answer: b) Entschuldigung, das ist kalt.

24. How do you ask to replace something?

a) Könnten Sie das bitte umtauschen?

b) Können wir die Rechnung haben?

c) Das Essen war hervorragend!

d) Ist das scharf?

Answer: a) Könnten Sie das bitte umtauschen?

25. What does "die Speisekarte" mean?

a) The menu

b) The waiter

c) The dessert

d) The tip

Answer: a) The menu

ᗊᗊᗊ

SIX

100 MOST COMMON VOCABULARY

The following is a comprehensive list of the 100 most common vocabulary words in the German language. Understanding these words is essential for anyone looking to learn German, as they form the foundation of everyday communication. Whether you are a beginner or looking to refresh your knowledge, this list will be valuable.

Common Vocabulary List

der (the - masculine)

die (the - feminine)

das (the - neuter)

und (and)

sein (to be)

haben (to have)

ich (I)

du (you - informal)

er (he)

sie (she)

es (it)

wir (we)

ihr (you - plural informal)

sie (they)

Sie (you - formal)

nicht (not)

ja (yes)

nein (no)

vielleicht (maybe)

aber (but)

oder (or)

weil (because)

wenn (if/when)

wo (where)

was (what)

wer (who)

wie (how)

warum (why)

jetzt (now)

heute (today)

morgen (tomorrow)

gestern (yesterday)

immer (always)

manchmal (sometimes)

nie (never)

viel (much/a lot)

wenig (little/few)

mehr (more)

weniger (less)

gut (good)

schlecht (bad)

groß (big)

klein (small)

lang (long)

kurz (short)

schön (beautiful)

hässlich (ugly)

neu (new)

alt (old)

teuer (expensive)

billig (cheap)

wichtig (important)

einfach (easy)

schwer (difficult)

schnell (fast)

langsam (slow)

heiß (hot)

kalt (cold)

warm (warm)

freundlich (friendly)

traurig (sad)

glücklich (happy)

müde (tired)

hungrig (hungry)

durstig (thirsty)

gesund (healthy)

krank (sick)

arbeiten (to work)

lernen (to learn)

spielen (to play)

essen (to eat)

trinken (to drink)

gehen (to go)

kommen (to come)

sehen (to see)

hören (to hear)

sprechen (to speak)

sagen (to say)

fragen (to ask)

antworten (to answer)

lieben (to love)

mögen (to like)

brauchen (to need)

denken (to think)

wissen (to know)

verstehen (to understand)

fühlen (to feel)

schlafen (to sleep)

stehen (to stand)

sitzen (to sit)

liegen (to lie)

fahren (to drive/go)

laufen (to run)

bringen (to bring)

nehmen (to take)

geben (to give)

zeigen (to show)

finden (to find)

verlieren (to lose)

beginnen (to begin)

This vocabulary list is a great starting point for anyone interested in learning German. Familiarizing yourself with these words will enhance your ability to communicate effectively in various situations.

Happy learning!

Multiple-Choice Questions on Common German Vocabulary

1. Which is the correct German definite article for a masculine noun?
a) die
b) das
c) der
d) ein
Answer: c) der

2. What is the German word for "they"?
a) ihr
b) wir
c) sie
d) er
Answer: c) sie

3. Which of these words means "you" in formal German?
a) du
b) ihr
c) Sie
d) sie
Answer: c) Sie

4. What is the German pronoun for "we"?
a) wir
b) ihr
c) er
d) sie
Answer: a) wir

5. Which of the following is NOT a German pronoun?
a) ich
b) er
c) das
d) sie
Answer: c) das

6. What is the German verb for "to have"?
a) sein

b) haben

c) machen

d) gehen

Answer: b) haben

7. How do you say "to be" in German?

a) wissen

b) nehmen

c) sein

d) gehen

Answer: c) sein

8. What does "gehen" mean in English?

a) to sit

b) to go

c) to stand

d) to run

Answer: b) to go

9. Which verb means "to eat" in German?

a) trinken

b) essen

c) schlafen

d) lernen

Answer: b) essen

10. What does the German verb "mögen" mean?

a) to like

b) to love

c) to sleep

d) to play

Answer: a) to like

11. What is the German word for "what"?

a) wo

b) was

c) wie

d) warum

Answer: b) was

12. How do you say "why" in German?

a) wie

b) wann

c) warum

d) wo

Answer: c) warum

13. Which German word means "where"?

a) wann

b) wo

c) wie

d) was

Answer: b) wo

14. What is the German equivalent of "when"?

a) warum

b) wann

c) wie

d) wo

Answer: b) wann

15. How do you say "sometimes" in German?

a) immer

b) nie

c) vielleicht

d) manchmal

Answer: d) manchmal

16. Which of the following means "big" in German?

a) klein

b) groß

c) kurz

d) lang

Answer: b) groß

17. How do you say "beautiful" in German?

a) hässlich

b) alt

c) schön

d) groß

Answer: c) schön

18. Which German word means "expensive"?

a) billig

b) teuer

c) gesund

d) müde

Answer: b) teuer

19. How do you say "fast" in German?

a) langsam

b) schnell

c) schwer

d) einfach

Answer: b) schnell

20. Which of the following means "cold" in German?

a) heiß

b) warm

c) kalt

d) schnell

Answer: c) kalt

21. How do you say "a lot" in German?

a) wenig

b) viel

c) mehr

d) vielleicht

Answer: b) viel

22. Which German word means "less"?

a) weniger

b) mehr

c) groß

d) lang

Answer: a) weniger

23. What does "gesund" mean in English?

a) happy

b) tired

c) healthy

d) important

Answer: c) healthy

24. Which German word means "tired"?

a) müde

b) hungrig

c) durstig

d) traurig

Answer: a) müde

25. What does "krank" mean in English?

a) sick

b) sad

c) sleepy

d) happy

Answer: a) sick

ϷϷϷ

SEVEN
100 Commonly Used Sentences

Common Greetings and Introductions

Hallo! – Hello!

Guten Morgen! – Good morning!

Guten Tag! – Good day!

Guten Abend! – Good evening!

Gute Nacht! – Good night!

Wie geht's? – How are you?

Mir geht's gut, danke. – I'm fine, thank you.

Wie heißen Sie? – What is your name? (formal)

Ich heiße... – My name is...

Freut mich, Sie kennenzulernen. – Nice to meet you. (formal)

Basic Questions

Wo ist die Toilette? – Where is the bathroom?

Was ist das? – What is that?

Wie viel kostet das? – How much does that cost?

Sprechen Sie Englisch? – Do you speak English? (formal)

Können Sie das bitte wiederholen? – Can you please repeat that?

Was machen Sie beruflich? – What do you do for a living? (formal)

Woher kommen Sie? – Where are you from? (formal)

Was ist Ihr Lieblingsessen? – What is your favorite food? (formal)

Haben Sie Geschwister? – Do you have siblings? (formal)

Was sind Ihre Hobbys? – What are your hobbies? (formal)

Everyday Conversations

Ich verstehe nicht. – I don't understand.

Können Sie langsamer sprechen? – Can you speak more slowly?

Ich bin verloren. – I am lost.

Ich habe Hunger. – I am hungry.

Ich habe Durst. – I am thirsty.

Ich bin müde. – I am tired.

Es tut mir leid. – I'm sorry.

Kein Problem. – No problem.

Ich mag das. – I like that.

Ich mag es nicht. – I don't like it.

Directions and Locations

Gehen Sie geradeaus. – Go straight.

Biegen Sie rechts ab. – Turn right.

Biegen Sie links ab. – Turn left.

Es ist in der Nähe. – It is nearby.

Es ist weit weg. – It is far away.

Ich suche... – I am looking for...

Ist das weit von hier? – Is it far from here?

Wo ist der nächste Bahnhof? – Where is the nearest train station?

Wo kann ich ein Taxi finden? – Where can I find a taxi?

Gibt es hier ein Restaurant? – Is there a restaurant here?

Shopping and Dining

Ich hätte gerne... – I would like...

Die Rechnung, bitte. – The bill, please.

Haben Sie eine Speisekarte auf Englisch? – Do you have a menu in English?

Ich bin allergisch gegen... – I am allergic to...

Kann ich mit Kreditkarte bezahlen? – Can I pay with a credit card?

Ich nehme das. – I'll take that.

Gibt es einen Rabatt? – Is there a discount?

Wo ist die nächste Apotheke? – Where is the nearest pharmacy?

Ich möchte etwas kaufen. – I want to buy something.

Das ist zu teuer. – That is too expensive.

Travel and Transportation

Ich brauche ein Ticket nach... – I need a ticket to...

Wann fährt der nächste Zug? – When does the next train leave?

Wo ist die Haltestelle? – Where is the bus stop?

Wie lange dauert die Fahrt? – How long does the journey take?

Ich möchte ein Zimmer reservieren. – I would like to book a room.

Haben Sie ein Zimmer frei? – Do you have a room available?

Ich habe eine Reservierung. – I have a reservation.

Wo kann ich ein Auto mieten? – Where can I rent a car?

Gibt es einen Flughafen in der Nähe? – Is there an airport nearby?

Ich bin mit dem Flugzeug hier. – I am here by plane.

Emergency Situations

Hilfe! – Help!

Rufen Sie die Polizei! – Call the police!

Ich brauche einen Arzt. – I need a doctor.

Wo ist das nächste Krankenhaus? – Where is the nearest hospital?

Ich habe meine Tasche verloren. – I lost my bag.

Ich wurde bestohlen. – I was robbed.

Ist alles in Ordnung? – Is everything okay?

Ich fühle mich nicht gut. – I don't feel well.

Können Sie mir helfen? – Can you help me?

Ich brauche einen Übersetzer. – I need a translator.

Socializing and Making Plans

Möchten Sie etwas trinken gehen? – Would you like to go for a drink?

Haben Sie Zeit, um sich zu treffen? – Do you have time to meet?

Was halten Sie von… ? – What do you think of…?

Ich lade Sie ein. – I invite you.

Lass uns ins Kino gehen. – Let's go to the cinema.

Ich freue mich darauf. – I am looking forward to it.

Wann haben Sie Zeit? – When do you have time?

Wo wollen wir uns treffen? – Where shall we meet?

Ich habe schon Pläne. – I already have plans.

Es war schön, Sie zu treffen. – It was nice to meet you.

Expressing Opinions and Feelings

Ich denke, dass... – I think that...

Ich glaube, dass... – I believe that...

Ich bin glücklich. – I am happy.

Ich bin traurig. – I am sad.

Ich bin aufgeregt. – I am excited.

Ich bin enttäuscht. – I am disappointed.

Ich fühle mich wohl. – I feel good.

Ich bin nervös. – I am nervous.

Ich bin zufrieden. – I am satisfied.

Ich bin stolz auf... – I am proud of...

Closing Conversations

Es war nett, mit Ihnen zu sprechen. – It was nice talking to you. (formal)

Ich muss jetzt gehen. – I have to go now.

Bis bald! – See you soon!

Tschüss! – Bye!

Auf Wiedersehen! – Goodbye!

Ich wünsche Ihnen einen schönen Tag! – I wish you a nice day!

Passen Sie auf sich auf! – Take care!

Viel Spaß! – Have fun!

Gute Reise! – Safe travels!

Bis zum nächsten Mal! – Until next time!

The above sentence list can be a foundational tool for anyone looking to communicate effectively in German. Practice these phrases regularly to build confidence and fluency in your conversations.

Multiple Type Questions

1. What does "Guten Abend!" mean in English?

a) Good morning

b) Good night

c) Good evening

d) Good afternoon

Answer: c) Good evening

2. How do you formally ask someone's name in German?

a) Wie heißt du?

b) Wie heißen Sie?

c) Wie geht's?

d) Was ist Ihr Name?

Answer: b) Wie heißen Sie?

3. What is the correct response to "Wie geht's?" if you are doing well?

a) Es tut mir leid.

b) Ich bin müde.

c) Mir geht's gut, danke.

d) Ich habe Hunger.

Answer: c) Mir geht's gut, danke.

4. Which phrase means "Where is the bathroom?"

a) Woher kommen Sie?

b) Was ist Ihr Lieblingsessen?

c) Wo ist die Toilette?

d) Haben Sie Geschwister?

Answer: c) Wo ist die Toilette?

5. How do you ask if someone speaks English formally?

a) Sprichst du Englisch?

b) Sprechen Sie Englisch?

c) Können Sie das bitte wiederholen?

d) Was ist das?

Answer: b) Sprechen Sie Englisch?

6. What does "Wie viel kostet das?" mean?

a) How much does that cost?

b) What is your name?

c) Where are you from?

d) Do you have siblings?

Answer: a) How much does that cost?

7. How do you say "I don't understand" in German?

a) Ich habe Durst.

b) Ich verstehe nicht.

c) Ich bin verloren.

d) Ich habe Hunger.

Answer: b) Ich verstehe nicht.

8. What phrase would you use if you need someone to speak slower?

a) Es tut mir leid.

b) Ich bin müde.

c) Ich mag das.

d) Können Sie langsamer sprechen?

Answer: d) Können Sie langsamer sprechen?

9. What does "Kein Problem" mean?

a) No problem

b) I am sorry

c) I don't like that

d) I am hungry

Answer: a) No problem

10. What is the German phrase for "Turn right"?

a) Gehen Sie geradeaus.

b) Biegen Sie links ab.

c) Biegen Sie rechts ab.

d) Wo ist der nächste Bahnhof?

Answer: c) Biegen Sie rechts ab.

11. If something is nearby, how would you say it in German?

a) Es ist weit weg.

b) Es ist in der Nähe.

c) Ich suche...

d) Wo kann ich ein Taxi finden?

Answer: b) Es ist in der Nähe.

12. How do you ask, "Where is the nearest train station?"

a) Wo kann ich ein Taxi finden?

b) Ist das weit von hier?

c) Wo ist der nächste Bahnhof?

d) Gibt es hier ein Restaurant?

Answer: c) Wo ist der nächste Bahnhof?

13. How do you ask for the bill in German?

a) Ich hätte gerne...

b) Die Rechnung, bitte.

c) Ich nehme das.

d) Gibt es einen Rabatt?

Answer: b) Die Rechnung, bitte.

14. What would you say to indicate you are allergic to something?

a) Ich bin allergisch gegen...

b) Ich habe Durst.

c) Kann ich mit Kreditkarte bezahlen?

d) Ich nehme das.

Answer: a) Ich bin allergisch gegen...

15. What does "Das ist zu teuer" mean?

a) I want to buy something.

b) This is too expensive.

c) Is there a discount?

d) I would like that.

Answer: b) This is too expensive.

16. How do you ask for a ticket to a place?

a) Ich brauche ein Ticket nach...

b) Wann fährt der nächste Zug?

c) Ich möchte ein Zimmer reservieren.

d) Ich habe eine Reservierung.

Answer: a) Ich brauche ein Ticket nach...

17. How do you ask about the duration of a journey?

a) Wo ist die Haltestelle?

b) Wie lange dauert die Fahrt?

c) Gibt es einen Flughafen in der Nähe?

d) Ich bin mit dem Flugzeug hier.

Answer: b) Wie lange dauert die Fahrt?

18. What does "Ich möchte ein Zimmer reservieren" mean?

a) I would like to book a room.

b) I have a reservation.

c) Do you have a room available?

d) Where can I rent a car?

Answer: a) I would like to book a room.

19. What is the German word for "Help!"?

a) Hilfe!

b) Es tut mir leid.

c) Ich brauche einen Arzt.

d) Ich wurde bestohlen.

Answer: a) Hilfe!

20. If you need a doctor, what would you say?

a) Ich fühle mich nicht gut.

b) Rufen Sie die Polizei!

c) Ich brauche einen Arzt.

d) Ich habe meine Tasche verloren.

Answer: c) Ich brauche einen Arzt.

21. What does "Ich lade Sie ein" mean?

a) I invite you.

b) I am hungry.

c) I have a reservation.

d) I have plans.

Answer: a) I invite you.

22. How do you ask "Where shall we meet?"

a) Wann haben Sie Zeit?

b) Wo wollen wir uns treffen?

c) Möchten Sie etwas trinken gehen?

d) Ich freue mich darauf.

Answer: b) Wo wollen wir uns treffen?

23. How do you say "I am happy" in German?

a) Ich bin traurig.

b) Ich bin glücklich.

c) Ich bin müde.

d) Ich bin enttäuscht.

Answer: b) Ich bin glücklich.

24. What does "Ich bin stolz auf..." mean?

a) I am proud of...

b) I am nervous.

c) I am tired.

d) I am disappointed.

Answer: a) I am proud of...

25. What is the correct phrase for "Take care!" in German?

a) Passen Sie auf sich auf!

b) Bis bald!

c) Gute Reise!

d) Ich muss jetzt gehen.

Answer: a) Passen Sie auf sich auf!

 DDD

Scan Here
FOR QUALITY BOOKS
For Home Library for
Parents, Educators &Students